; WEIST III
'VANITY"

TE MEDIA GROUP, LLC

CPSIA information can be obtained
at www.ICGtesting.com
Printed in the USA
LVHW081952250821
696087LV00020B/1446/J

9 780578 822457